# Don't Feed the Dog!

**D**anny hate**d** sandwiches.
His **Da<u>dd</u>**y always put che**dd**ar cheese
sandwiches in his lunchbox.

Every **d**ay **D**anny brought his che**dd**ar sandwiches home from school and fe**d** them to their **d**og calle**d** Te**dd**y.

One **d**ay **D**a**dd**y saw from a window **D**anny fee**d**ing Te**dd**y his sandwiches. He was so ma**d**!

He stomped outsi**de** **–d-d-d-d-d-d-d-d-d**-.
His feet soun**ded** like thunder!

"**D**anny! **D**on't fee**d** the **d**og!
He will get fat," sai**d** **D**a**dd**y.

But **D**anny **did**n't listen. He hi**d** his che**dd**ar sandwiches under his be**d** and snuck Te**dd**y into his room to secretly fee**d** him.

**D**ays went by and weeks and even months and **D**a**dd**y still **did**n't know **D**anny's secret.

Te**dd**y got fatter and fatter…

And bigger and bigger...

Until he was the fattest **d**og **D**a**dd**y ha**d** ever seen!

**D**a**dd**y coul**d**n't understand why Te**dd**y ha**d** got so fat. And so hungry!

One **d**ay a hungry Te**dd**y went into **D**anny's room to find the sandwiches by himself.

**D**a**dd**y looked outsi**d**e and saw something funny...

Te**dd**y was waddling to his kennel with sandwiches in his mouth!

**D**a**dd**y stomped madly to find **D**anny
**–d-d-d-d-d-d-d-d-d-d-d-.**

"**D**anny, I told you not to fee**d** Te**dd**y.
Look how fat he is!"

**D**anny's secret was found out.
He was in a lot of trouble!

He ha**d** no choice. He ha**d** to eat his sandwiches.
The more he ate, the easier it got.

The easier it got, the better the sandwiches taste**d**.
Soon he liked eating his sandwiches!

Te**dd**y shrunk back to his normal size again.
But he sure missed those sandwiches!